FOLLOW ME

JoAnne Nelson
Pictures by Mark Anthony

PRICE STERN SLOAN

Los Angeles

DEVELOPMENTAL EDITOR: Diane Arnell
PROJECT EDITOR: Judith E. Nayer
DESIGN & PRODUCTION: Thomasina Webb
ART DIRECTION: Bob Feldgus
MEDIA EDITOR: Glenn E. Conner
MUSIC COMPOSITION/PRODUCTION: Michael Lobel

ISBN: 0-8431-2493-8
10   9   8   7   6   5   4   3   2   1

I went for a walk
and what did I see?

A little red puppy
was following me.

I went for a walk
and what did I see?

A fluffy orange kitten
was following me.

I went for a walk
and what did I see?

A pretty blue bird
was following me.

I went for a walk
and what did I see?

A jumping green frog
was following me.

I went for a walk
and what did I see?

A soft yellow duckling
was following me.

I went for a walk
and what did I see?

A round purple bug
was following me.

When I got home, what did I see?
They all came in
and had lunch with me.

16